Documenting History

Documenting World War I

Philip Steele

New York

Published in 2010 by The Rosen Publishing Group Inc.
29 East 21st Street, New York, NY 10010

First Edition

Senior editor: Camilla Lloyd
Designer: Phipps Design
Consultant: Dr. Andrew Dilley
Picture researcher: Shelley Noronha
Indexer and proofreader: Cath Senker

Library of Congress Cataloging-in-Publication Data

Steele, Philip, 1948-
 Documenting World War I / Philip Steele. -- 1st ed.
    p. cm. -- (Documenting history)
 Includes index.
 ISBN 978-1-4358-9673-4 (library binding)
 ISBN 978-1-4358-9674-1 (paperback)
 ISBN 978-1-4358-9681-9 (6-pack)
 1. World War, 1914-1918--Sources--Juvenile literature. I. Title.
 D522.7.S745 2010
 940.3--dc22
                                2009026077

Photo Credits:
The author and publisher would like to thank the following for allowing their pictures to
be reproduced in this publication: Cover: Main and background: Wayland Picture Library,
BL: Getty Images; 1 Wayland Picture Library, 5 Wayland Picture Library, 6 © Hulton-
Deutsch Collection/CORBIS, 7 Wayland Picture Library, 8 © Bettmann/ CORBIS, 9 popper-
foto/ Getty Images, 10 © 2004 Credit: Topham Picturepoint, 11 akg-images, 13, 14 & 15
Wayland Picture Library, 16 ©2003 Credit:Topham Picturepoint, 17 Hulton Archive/Getty
Images,18 © CORBIS,19 TopFoto, 20 © Lebrecht Music & Arts/Corbis, 21 ©Ullstein
Bild/TopFoto, 22 Hulton Archive/Getty Images, 23 Wayland Picture Library, 24 akg-images,
25 ©2005 Credit:TopFoto, 26 Hulton Archive/Getty Images, 27 Illustrated London
News/Mary Evans Picture Library, 28 Wayland Picture Library, 29 Getty Images, 30 Hulton
Archive/Getty Images, 31 akg-images/Columbia Pictures, 32 Wayland Picture Library, 33
Mary Evans Picture Library/Rue Des Archives, 34 © Swim Ink 2,LLC/CORBIS, 35, 36
Wayland Picture Library, 37 © Bettmann/CORBIS, 38, 39 Wayland Picture Library, 40 ©
Hulton-Deutsch Collection/CORBIS, 41 Topfoto, 42, 43 Hulton Archive/Getty Images, 44 ©
Ric Ergenbright/CORBIS.

Manufactured in China

CPSIA Compliance Information: Batch #WAW0102YA: For Further Information
contact Rosen Publishing, New York, New York at 1-800-237-9932

CONTENTS

The Great War

Until World War II broke out in 1939, World War I was simply known as "the Great War." It needed no other explanation. This conflict, which lasted from July 28, 1914 to November 11, 1918, shocked the world and changed the lives of millions of people. Its memory hung heavily over every country in the 1920s and 1930s.

The conflict eventually became better known as a *world war*, because it

had involved troops from around the globe—from Europe, Asia, Africa, the Americas, and Oceania. At that time, the most powerful European nations ruled vast overseas empires, whose peoples were drawn into the conflict. Most of the fighting took place in Europe and the Middle East, with some in Africa and the Pacific.

World War I (WWI) was documented with newspaper articles, cartoons, photographs, paintings, poems, silent movies, and early sound recordings, as well as official papers, army reports,

This map shows nations with their dates of entry into World War I. The two sides became known as the Allied or Entente Forces and the opposing Central Powers.

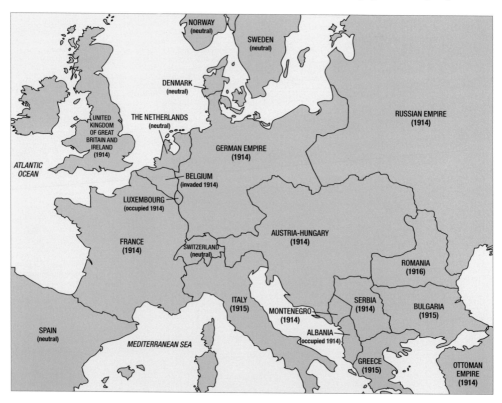

debates in governments and official histories. Why do we need to study them and what can we learn from them?

The war changed the course of the twentieth century. It destroyed nations and created new ones. It triggered political revolutions and uprisings, and played a part in great social changes, such as improved rights and votes for women. It created many economic problems and sowed the seeds of World War II (1939–45).

New weapons and methods of warfare changed forever the way in which wars are fought, and posed new ethical dilemmas for humanity. Soldiers were poisoned with gas. Civilians were bombed from the air. The number of soldiers killed was on a scale never known before.

The political troubles in today's Middle East, and in the Balkans, all point back to WWI. So, too, do the activities of today's United Nations, for it was out of that first global conflict that there came attempts to build a new world order based on international law, through a treaty organization called the League of Nations.

However, another reason to find out about WWI is more personal. The conflict and its aftermath left few families untouched. Women were widowed, girls never married, children were orphaned. Many families still have personal documents—letters, diaries, and postcards—which tell these moving stories.

Countries in World War I (1914–18)

ALLIED/ENTENTE FORCES

- Belgium and colonies from 1914
- British Empire—Australia, British Crown Colonies, Canada, India, New Zealand, Newfoundland, South Africa, United Kingdom (including Ireland) from 1914
- French Republic and French colonies from 1914
- Greece from 1915
- Italy from 1915
- Japan from 1914
- Montenegro and Serbia from 1914
- Portugal and Portuguese colonies from 1916
- Romania from 1916
- Russian Empire from 1914 to November 1917
- Plus 20 other nations
- U.S.A. (Associate Power) from 1917

CENTRAL POWERS

- Austria-Hungary from 1914
- German Empire and German colonies from 1914
- Ottoman (Turkish) Empire from 1914
- Bulgaria from 1915

To the brink

In 1900, the nations of Europe were bound together by treaties and by political and economic alliances. The powerful royal families of Britain, Germany, and Russia were closely related to each other. Surely such binding connections would ensure peace? There was a growing interest in education, science, and progress. So how did bright hopes for the new century descend so quickly into a catastrophic war?

The roots of WWI lay in the troubled politics and economics of nineteenth-century Europe. This was a period of rapid social and economic change, known as the Industrial Revolution. People from the countryside poured into the growing cities to work in new factories and mills. This new urban working class was largely excluded from the political system. The countries where these changes were taking place had no adequate political systems or constitutions in place to cope with the new social order.

Many of them were tiny states that had changed little since the Middle Ages. Nationalists struggled to create modern nations from a jigsaw puzzle

SOURCE

RECOLLECTION

"The German Emperor is aging me; he is like a battleship with steam up and screws going, but with no rudder, and he will run into something some day and cause a catastrophe."

Edward Grey, British Foreign Secretary from 1905–16, was describing German Kaiser Wilhelm II. Wilhelm was Queen Victoria's grandson. He was disabled and tried to prove himself by adopting militarist attitudes. However, he turned out to be a weak and blustering leader in wartime, dominated by his generals.

Edward Grey, 1st Viscount Grey of Fallodon (1862–1933).

Pomp and ceremony from another age: The German emperor, Kaiser Wilhelm II, rides to review his troops in the capital, Berlin, in 1912.

*The British battleship, **HMS Dreadnought**, launched in 1906, gave its name to a new class of ship. Other navies hurried to match its powerful new technology.*

of cities, principalities, duchies, and kingdoms. By 1871, both Italy and Germany had been united as single countries. However, the process of nation building was also a struggle, often a violent one, between liberals, calling for democratic reform, and military-minded conservatives who opposed change and were terrified of revolution. As a result, there was little political stability. Governments built up big armies to defend themselves. The Napoleonic Wars (1803–15) had set France against Britain and the German states.

In the Crimean War (1853–56), Britain, France, and Turkey had fought against Russia. In 1870, the German kingdom of Prussia had invaded France. Rivalry between European nations became global as they scrambled to create overseas empires in Africa, Asia, and the Pacific. Overseas colonies provided the raw materials and markets for Europe's new factory goods.

This heady mixture of nationalism and imperialism made the world a dangerous place. In the years before 1914, rivalries between a militaristic German government and other European powers nearly boiled over into war, for instance, in Morocco in 1905–6 and 1911. An arms race developed, as Germany greatly increased its armed forces, and Britain upgraded its battle fleet.

It was clear that Europe's foundations were resting on gunpowder. One spark, and a great explosion would follow.

Sarajevo 1914

The spark that set off WWI occurred when shots rang out in Sarajevo, the capital of Bosnia, on June 28, 1914. The heir to the Austrian throne, the Archduke Franz Ferdinand, and his wife Sophie, were assassinated by a Bosnian Serb nationalist named Gavrilo Princip, who was opposed to the expansion of rule in the region by Austria-Hungary.

Some Austrian politicians were determined to force a war with the Kingdom of Serbia. After Franz Ferdinand's death, Austria-Hungary, supported by militarist generals and politicians in Germany, made a series

Franz Ferdinand of Austria-Este (1863–1914) and his wife Sophie, before their assassination. The archduke was actually quite sympathetic to the Serbian cause.

of demands on Serbia. The Serbs agreed to all of these, except one—the terms of the investigation into the assassination. Austria-Hungary immediately declared war on Serbia. The Serbian people were Slavs, as were the Russians, so it was hardly surprising that Russia backed Serbia. France supported Russia, which was its ally. Germany now declared war on Russia and France.

Germany's war plan was to start by launching an immediate surprise attack on France, through the small country of Belgium. Belgium was neutral, not being part of any military alliance with the great powers. It refused to let the German army pass through its territory, but Germany

invaded anyway. Britain was bound by treaty to support Belgian neutrality. On the following day, August 4, 1914, the United Kingdom of Great Britain and Ireland declared war on Germany.

In October 1914, Turkish ships attacked Russian seaports along the Black Sea coast. The Ottoman empire, which included Turkey and large areas of southeastern Europe and Western Asia, had entered the war on the side of Germany and Austria-Hungary. A year later, Bulgaria joined the same alliance.

Gavrilo Princip, the 19-year-old gunman who triggered the war, is arrested in Sarajevo in 1914. He died in prison in 1918.

SOURCE

TELEGRAM

"Am glad you are back. In this serious moment, I appeal to you to help me. An ignoble war has been declared to a weak country. The indignation in Russia shared fully by me is enormous. I foresee that very soon I shall be overwhelmed by the pressure forced upon me and be forced to take extreme measures which will lead to war. To try and avoid such a calamity as a European war, I beg you in the name of our old friendship to do what you can to stop your allies from going too far."

Tsar Nicholas II is sending a telegram to his cousin Kaiser Wilhelm II. "The weak country" to which he refers is Serbia. The "allies" are the Austro-Hungarians.

From Tsar Nicholas II of Russia to Kaiser Wilhelm II. July 29, 1914, 1 a.m.
Peter's Court Palais, July 29, 1914, Sa Majesté l'Empereur—Neues Palais.

The two sides in the war would be known by various names. The alliance between France, Britain, and Russia was known as the Triple Entente. As more countries joined, they were known together as the Entente Powers or the Allies. The alliance between Germany, Austria-Hungary, and the Ottoman empire was called the Triple Alliance. This full group of nations became known as the Central Powers.

The treaties that were supposed to guarantee the security of Europe dragged the whole continent into war. Other countries around the edge of the conflict waited to see how they might best benefit from taking part, and on which side.

Patriotism and propaganda

The troops that marched to war in 1914 sang popular songs and were cheered by crowds. Many were country boys who had never seen the wider world. This was to be an exciting and heroic adventure. It was said that the war would be over by Christmas. Posters called on young men to volunteer for the armed forces.

The war actually lasted more than four years. By 1916, 3 million volunteers had joined up in the United Kingdom alone. The majority of people felt deeply patriotic.

A poster calls on the "Young Lions" of the British empire to support the "Old Lion" of the United Kingdom in its battle with Germany.

SOURCE

POSTCARD

"Hats off to the Flag we all love and adore,

And give it a mighty cheer,

For with gallant commanders like these to the fore—

Old England has nothing to fear."

This poem was featured on a card with a photograph of British Admiral Sir John Jellicoe, and drawings of a battleship, an airplane and a gun. It was mailed from London to a child staying in Littlehampton, Sussex, on September 11, 1914.

THE EMPIRE NEEDS MEN!

THE OVERSEAS STATES

All answer the call.
Helped by the YOUNG LIONS
The OLD LION defies his Foes
ENLIST NOW.

Individuals who did not volunteer risked being publicly shamed, and being handed white feathers (a symbol of cowardice) by women loyalists. After 1916, unmarried men between 18 and 41 were forcibly conscripted, for the first time in British history.

Not all went willingly. Conscientious objectors refused to fight on principle. Some were pacifists, who believed that taking life was immoral. Some of them agreed to work in nonviolent support roles, but others refused any part in the war. They could be imprisoned, or forcibly sent to the front, where they could be shot if they disobeyed orders.

Communists and some moderate socialists from all countries were opposed to the war on political grounds. They believed that this conflict was about imperialism and the control of global markets, and was not being fought in the interests of the working class. However, the majority of working-class movements in Europe did end up supporting the war.

Not all citizens were loyal. Some French Canadians were reluctant to volunteer to fight for the English-speaking government in Ottawa. Irish nationalists secretly negotiated German support and in 1916, rose up against British rule in Dublin. This "Easter Rising" was crushed, but marked the start of a process that eventually led to Irish independence. Within the Ottoman empire, the Turkish government fought an Arab revolt and massacred over a million Armenians, whom they accused of sympathizing with the enemy.

Jingoism, an extreme form of patriotism, was common. The popular press whipped up a storm of xenophobia. A British journalist, Horatio Bottomley, denounced the "Huns" (Germans) as subhumans who should be exterminated. A German politician, Matthias Erzberger, declared it would be better to kill the population

LA PUISSANCE MILITAIRE DE LA FRANCE

SOURCE

POSTER

Posters were used for patriotic propaganda. This one glorifies the "military might of France." It shows a French biplane forcing down a German aircraft.

of London than to shed the blood of one German soldier. In England, loyal British people of German descent were bullied and forced to change their names. Even the British royal family felt it wise to Anglicize their name from Wettin to Windsor.

The long struggle

In August 1914, German troops pushed westward toward Paris. Their "Schlieffen plan" aimed to defeat France quickly in the west, before Russia could mobilize in the east. However, in September 1914, they were halted by British and French armies along the River Marne, in a battle involving about two million troops.

The Germans were then forced to retreat 40 miles (65 km), where they dug in by making trenches. So did the Allies. A twin line of trenches soon stretched from the coast of the English Channel to the Swiss border, passing through Belgium and France. Between them lay "no man's land," a contested wasteland of barbed wire and mud, raked by gunfire and pounded by shells.

Each side tried to break through the enemy lines. Artillery bombarded enemy positions, then troops would advance and try to capture enemy trenches. The Verdun offensive, launched by the Germans in 1916, caused 600,000 deaths, and achieved little. The first offensive on the River Somme was launched by British and

French troops from July to November 1916, to win just 5 miles (8 km) of land. In this short period, more than 1,043,000 soldiers from both sides were killed. The Germans regrouped behind a series of defenses called the Hindenburg line.

This map shows the position of the Western Front in 1915. The Central Powers pushed far into France but failed to reach Paris.

Key

Under control of Entente forces (Allies)

Under control of Central Powers

The French-led Nivelle offensive in 1917 failed. At the Messines ridge, the British dug tunnels filled with explosives under German lines, killing 10,000 of the enemy. An attempt to break through to the Belgian coast on the Passchendaele ridge led to the

Allied troops file up a trench to launch an attack across no man's land. As soon as they left their positions, they were exposed to enemy machine-gun fire.

slaughter of 570,00 Allied troops and Germans. The war was by now costing Britain alone £7 million ($13 million) a day. In the spring of 1918, the Germans pushed west once more, reaching the River Marne for the first time since 1914. However, new troops were arriving in support of the Allies from the U.S.A. (see pages 34–35).

The bravery shown on the Western Front was extraordinary. So, too, was the massive loss of life. Could the high casualty rates have been avoided? Some historians declare that the generals could do little in the face of a static war and devastating new weaponry. Other historians have blamed generals on all sides for using their troops as cannon fodder. Comparisons were made with the Crimean War, when it had been claimed that British troops were "lions led by donkeys."

SOURCE

LETTER

"We had to dig ourselves into holes on the Thursday night, but fortunately got well dug in before Fritz [Germans] began shelling us. He piled over some odd thousands of shells that night, and we lost a few men. I had six of my platoon buried, but four of them got out. Then on Friday morning, our guns opened, and Fritz came back with the worst artillery duel ever put on this front, so they tell us. We lay flat in our holes, until 9 a.m. when we had to pull out to support the front line, and it was some little hell getting up through a foot of mud and water …"

Letter from Canadian soldier Andrew Wilson to his wife, Monica, November 14, 1917, Western Front.
With the permission of The Canadian Letters and Images Project (www.canadianletters.ca).

Life and death in the trenches

Behind the front line on both sides were the heavily shelled ruins of towns, villages, and farmhouses. There were field hospitals with nurses, army camps, and lines of wounded soldiers, horses, wagons, and motor vehicles. Soldiers would wait here in reserve or on support duties, before being sent up for a period on the front line.

Exhausted troops take a break in the Allied trenches on the Western Front.

The dugouts (shelters in the soil), were linked by a network of trenches, filled with stinking mud and foul water, and overrun with rats. Disease was rife. Trench foot rotted the toes; body lice brought trench fever. Death was everywhere. One careless look over the parapet and a sniper's bullet would bring instant death. Periscopes had to be used to view the enemy positions. Shells—"whizz-bangs"—would cause random terror, leaving great craters in which a man could drown. Troops fired at the enemy from a firestep (a ledge) at the front of the trench. For an offensive, the troops would be led "over the top" into no man's land, risking death from machine-gun fire, explosives, and barbed wire.

The day was exhausting, starting before dawn. Those who were not

SONG

"*If you want to find the old battalion,
I know where they are, I know where they are.
If you want to find the old battalion,
I know where they are,
They're hanging on the old barbed wire.
I've seen 'em, I've seen 'em,
Hanging on the old barbed wire …*"

This is the last verse of *If You Want to Find the Sergeant-Major*. The words of this song were made up by British soldiers in the trenches. The previous battalion (fighting unit) has been machine-gunned on the barbed wire.

fighting were rebuilding fortifications, carrying messages, or rescuing the wounded on stretchers. Soldiers who fell asleep while keeping watch on sentry duty could be court-martialed and shot. Troops suffering from trauma, known as shell shock, often lost control and found themselves accused of cowardice or desertion, for which the penalty was also death.

Stress could be extreme, and was only relieved by writing home, by singing humorous or sentimental songs, by playing the mouth organ, or smoking tobacco. German soldiers were nicknamed "Fritz." British soldiers were known as "Tommies," and the French as *Poilus* (meaning "hairy ones"). Australians were "Diggers." Sometimes there would be informal truces. At Christmas 1914, some German troops began to sing carols, and the Tommies joined in. Both sides came out of the trenches and played soccer in no man's land. A similar incident happened between French and German troops in 1915.

Sometimes excessive discipline and exhaustion caused troops to mutiny (disobey orders). This happened among British empire troops at the Étaples camp in France in 1916, and among French troops during the Nivelle offensive of 1917.

SOURCE

MEMOIR

"From time to time, one of us disappeared up to their waist in the mud, and if our comrades had not come to their rescue, holding out their rifle butt, they would certainly have gone under. We ran along the rims of the shell-holes as if we were on a thin edge of honeycomb. Traces of blood on the surface of some heavy shell-holes told us that several men had already been swallowed up."

A German soldier, Ernst Jünger, was wounded on 14 occasions. He was among those troops on both sides who believed that combat brought out noble qualities in an individual.

Ernst Jünger, in *Stahlgewittern* (Storm of Steel, 1920).

British troops are inspected for trench foot. This condition could result in gangrene and amputation of the foot.

Clothes, guns, gas, and tanks

All kinds of uniforms could be seen on the Western Front, mostly in the drab colors necessary for camouflage in modern warfare—khaki for British empire troops, gray for the Germans, blue for the French. Legs were protected from the mud with cloth bindings called puttees. All kinds of headgear were to be seen, from the traditional German spiked *Pickelhaube* and various designs of peaked caps, to the turbans worn by Sikh troops in the Indian Army. Most important in the trenches were life-saving steel helmets. Officers wore knee-length riding boots and polished leather belts, with a revolver.

The standard weapon of the infantry was the repeating rifle, which had a bolt action to load bullets from a magazine. There was the British Lee-Enfield, the French Lebel, and the German Mauser. Bayonets could be fixed to the rifle for an assault. Flame-throwers wreaked havoc, as did machine guns that could pump out 600 bullets a minute. Artillery was of a size never seen before, firing new high explosive shells. Massive guns, mortars, and howitzers (a kind of cannon used

Machine-gunners wear gas masks near the village of Ovillers, during the Battle of the Somme in July 1916.

in sieges) were designed, such as the Germans' Big Bertha, or their Paris Gun, which had a range of 75 miles (120 kilometers).

One of the most dreadful new weapons was poison gas. A form of tear gas was first used by the French in 1914. Canisters of deadly chlorine gas were used by the Germans in April 1915, and their example was followed by the British that September. Later, phosgene and mustard gas were used. Poison gases killed many soldiers, or left them blinded or with damaged lungs. Often the wind blew the gas back over both sides in the battle. Basic gas masks were worn by troops and even by horses for protection.

This was the first war in which tanks were used. These tracked, armored monsters were invented by the British, and first appeared at Delville Wood in 1916. They were very hot and full of fumes, and often broke down, but they could tackle the mud and barbed wire head on. Tanks were used again by the French during the Aisne offensive, but the first real tank victory was at Cambrai in 1917, when 474 British tanks attacked the Hindenburg line. The first tank-to-tank battle took place at Villers Bretonneux in 1918, before a brutal infantry battle in which 1,200 Australians died.

SOURCE

POEM

"Gas! Gas! Quick, boys!—An ecstasy of fumbling,
Fitting the clumsy helmets just in time;
But someone still was yelling and stumbling
And floundering like a man in fire or lime—
Dim, through the misty panes and thick green light,
As under a green sea, I saw him drowning.

In all my dreams, before my helpless sight,
He plunges at me, guttering, choking, drowning …"

The English war poet, Wilfred Owen, describes the horrors of a poison gas attack.

Wilfred Owen, *Dulce et Decorum est*, 1917.

The British use of tanks at Cambrai in 1917 was a turning point in the history of warfare.

The war at sea

The sight of a huge naval fleet lined up for review on the gray waters of the North Sea, with funnels making smoke and flags fluttering, was the ultimate symbol of imperial power. The new heavily armored warships were powered by fast steam turbines and had massive firepower. For a hundred years, people had believed that whoever ruled the waves, ruled the world. However, this war was turning out to be quite different than expected, at sea as well as on land.

In August 1914, the imperial navies were stationed in many different parts of the world. As they repositioned after the outbreak of war, there were naval battles between Britain and Germany off Coronel in Chile, and off the Falkland, or Malvinas, Islands in the South Atlantic. Britain's big plan was

SOURCE

MEMOIR

"I saw that the bubble-track of the torpedo had been discovered on the bridge of the steamer, as frightened arms pointed toward the water and the captain put his hands in front of his eyes and waited resignedly. Then a frightful explosion followed, and we were all thrown against one another by the concussion ..."

A German U-boat captain recalls the horror of a torpedo attack on a British ship in April 1916.

Extract from *U-Boat 202* by Adolf K. G. E. von Spiegel (1919). U-boat Attack, 1916, EyeWitness to History, www.eyewitnesstohistory.com, 1997.

A German U-boat surfaces. Submarine warfare threatened the entire Allied war effort, which depended on supplies reaching western Europe across the Atlantic Ocean.

to blockade the main German fleet in its ports, illegally mining international waters in the northern North Sea. The Germans never did manage to break out of the blockade. There was a huge sea battle off Jutland, Denmark, in 1916, but neither side could be said to have won.

Beneath the Atlantic Ocean, another kind of dangerous warfare was being fought for the first time, in the enclosed metal world of the submarine. During the war, Germany and Britain used submarines in the Baltic, the North Sea, the Atlantic Ocean, and the Mediterranean. Germany decided to use its U-boats to prevent supplies from North America reaching Britain. It targeted merchant ships and passenger ships as well as naval vessels, and in 1915, fired torpedoes (underwater explosive missiles) at a famous British liner called the *Lusitania*. The attack killed 1,198 people, including many women, children—and 128 U.S. citizens. International opinion turned against Germany, regarding this as a war crime. The attack eventually played a part in bringing the United States into the war.

SOURCE

PAINTING

This oil painting by Robert H. Smith depicts the Battle of Jutland in 1916.

Various antisubmarine tactics were tried. Decoy vessels called Q-ships were used to lure U-boats within range, before revealing their hidden guns. In July 1916, the British began to use depth charges (explosive charges set off by pressure as they sink) to blast submarines underwater. In 1917, a system of convoys was developed, in which merchant ships gathered together to be escorted across the Atlantic by warships. U-boat attacks began to be less common.

War in the air

The first flight in a powered airplane was made in 1903 in the United States. Within just eight years, planes were being used in warfare. Aerial warfare developed further in WWI, with flying corps soon becoming separate branches of the armed forces.

Various types of aircraft were used, from hot air balloons to airships, which were cigar-shaped, gas-filled containers, either inflatable or rigid, with engines and a cabin. Airplanes were mostly tiny by modern standards. They were lightweight structures made of plywood and fabric, with a propeller and one, two, or three sets of wings (monoplanes, biplanes, or triplanes) linked by struts. Famous models used by the Germans included Fokker, Albatros, and Junkers. British names included Sopwith, Handley Page, and Armstrong. The French had the Nieuport and Breguet designs.

Planes were at first used mostly for reconnaissance. This meant they would fly over enemy lines looking for troop movements or weak defenses. They would also work with the artillery, spotting and identifying targets.

Fighter planes soon played a major role in the war, soaring high above the clouds and the battlefields below. At first, pilots were issued with handguns and grenades, but planes were soon fitted with machine guns. A gear was invented that allowed the gun to be coordinated with the propeller, so that it shot between the whirling blades.

SOURCE

POSTCARD

This German propaganda postcard imagines the bombing of Warsaw by an airship made by the Schutte-Lanz company, a competitor of the more famous Zeppelin.

Dogfights were aerial combats between fighter pilots in which the pilots twisted, turned, rolled, and looped. Pilots who brought down the most enemy aircraft became popular heroes, such as the German fighter ace, Baron Manfred von Richthofen. Aerial combat may have seemed romantic, but it was deadly. In April 1917, a British pilot on the Western Front could expect to survive for just 17.5 flying hours.

*The German pilot of a **Fokker DR1** triplane is strapped to his seat before take-off from a snowy airfield, in the last winter of the war.*

At first, all kinds of aircraft were used to drop bombs. Later, larger and more specialized aircraft were built for bombing. The Russians were the first to fit one plane with four engines. The first bombing of civilians took place in 1915, when Zeppelin airships from Germany dropped bombs on Norfolk, England. This was a small start to what would became a horrific problem of the twentieth century, as the aerial bombing of cities took place on an ever-increasing scale of terror.

SOURCE

MEMOIR

"When I started, the rain began falling. I had to throw away my goggles, otherwise I should not have seen anything. The trouble was that I had to travel over the mountains of the Moselle where the thunderstorm was just raging. I said to myself that probably I should be lucky and get through and rapidly approached the black cloud which reached down to the earth. I flew at the lowest possible altitude. I was compelled absolutely to leap over houses and trees with my machine. Very soon, I knew no longer where I was. The gale seized my machine as if it were a piece of paper and drove it along. My heart sank within me. I could not stand among the hills. I was compelled to go on."

The German fighter ace known as "The Red Baron" describes flying in a thunderstorm in 1916. His book was probably edited for German propaganda purposes. Before he died in 1917, Richthofen said that he disliked the tone of his book, and that his attitudes had changed.

Baron Manfred von Richthofen in *Der Rote Kampfflieger* (The Red Fighter Pilot), 1917.

From the Alps to Greece

While the long war dragged on in the muddy fields of France and Belgium, there was heavy fighting and loss of life on a very different front. Armies were being sent to the river valleys of what is now Slovenia, and to the snowy peaks, lakes, and forests of the Alps, along the border between Italy and Austria.

Italy had joined the war on the Allied side in April 1915, hoping to win back Italian-speaking lands in the far north from Austrian rule and gain territory on the Adriatic coast. Austria-Hungary now faced war not only with the Russians and Serbs in the east, but with the Italians in the south.

The Italians had large numbers of troops, but experienced problems with equipment and supply. The land was often mountainous and rough. Mules, bicycles, skis, and cable cars had to be used to move soldiers or supplies. There were specialist mountain troops (*Alpini*), and the light infantry units known as *Bersaglieri*, wearing distinctive plumes of cockerel feathers. Arms included Beretta pistols, Mannlicher-Carcano rifles, and Fiat-Revelli machine guns. The Italian air war was fought with Caproni bombers. Allied planes flew south over the Alps to support Italian offensives.

The infantry of Austria-Hungary wore gray-green uniforms and carried Mannlicher rifles. They, too, were often

Doctors treat patients at a Serbian field hospital. About 275,000 Serbian soldiers died during the war.

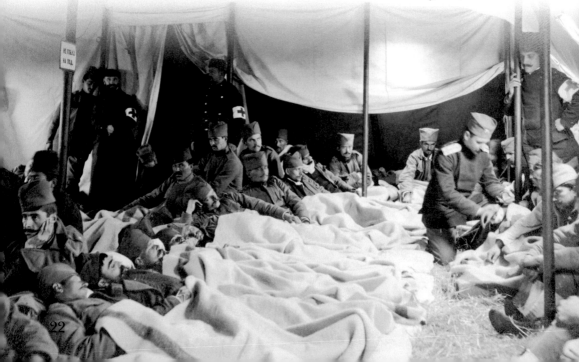

poorly equipped. They were conscripted from across the Austro-Hungarian empire. Although most officers were German-speakers, other ranks spoke many different Central European languages.

Italian troops march down from the mountains. Poorly equipped and trained, they were treated harshly by their own commanders and suffered heavy casualties.

Italy's war began with battles along the River Insonzo. In 1916, during the Asiago offensive, German troops were sent to reinforce the Austrians. October and November 1917 saw Italy crushed by the Central Powers at Caporetto (Kobarid, in Slovenia). The victors pushed south into Italy, but were held by Allied troops along the River Piave. An almighty Austro-Hungarian assault on the Piave in June 1918 failed. Time was now running out for the Austrians, whose empire had dominated much of Europe for many centuries.

Farther to the east lay the lands of southern Central Europe and the Balkan peninsula, where a series of ferocious wars had already occurred before 1914. Serbia held out against Austria-Hungary until defeat in late 1915. Bulgaria joined the Central Powers, and Romania and Greece joined the Allies. The war raged across both Slavic and Greek Macedonia. Losses were severe.

ADDRESS

"Soldiers! For months and months, resisting victoriously amidst the glaciers and the snows, accomplishing faithfully your duty in the tempests of winter, you have looked down upon the sunny plain of Italy.

The time to go down into it has come. Like the whirlwind, you will overthrow the false and perjured ally of the past, as well as the friends she has called to her help. You will prove to the world that nobody can resist your heroism."

Hötzendorf issued this statement before the Battle of the River Piave. His "whirlwind" failed, and the collapse of Habsburg rule followed shortly after.

General Count Franz Conrad von Hötzendorf, Austrian Commander-in-Chief on the Italian Front, June 14, 1918.

Cavalry and Bolsheviks

A great plain stretches from Germany, through Poland into Russia. It is hot in summer, but its bitterly cold winter climate has brought many armies to grief. To the south rise the Carpathian mountains and beyond them the River Danube. For centuries, Central Europe had been dominated or occupied by the Germans, the Russians, or the Austrians, which is why these regions formed a battle front in WWI. A fourth great power, the Ottoman empire of the Turks, lay to the southeast.

Fighting on the Eastern Front involved great movements of infantry, cavalry, and artillery. When the war started, Russia immediately sent a huge army westward. It was defeated by the Germans at Tannenberg. In the summer of 1915, the Germans pushed the Russians back 300 miles (480 kilometers). The Austro-Hungarian troops, farther south, struggled to hold back the enemy.

In 1915, Britain and France planned to force a route of support for the Russians through the "back door" of the Dardanelles, the Turkish strait that leads from the Aegean Sea to the Sea of Marmara. The Allied naval fleet was damaged in mined waters, and a landing was made on the heavily defended Gallipoli peninsula, with horrific losses. After nine months of trench warfare, the Allied troops had

to be evacuated, a major boost for Turkish morale. Many of the Allied force were "Anzacs" (members of the Australia and New Zealand Army Corps). The Gallipoli campaign became a landmark in the history of those two countries.

PAINTING

A painting recalls the devastation and death on the Eastern Front. Russia's Bolshevik government finally ended the war with Germany by the Treaty of Brest-Litovsk (March 1918).

On the Eastern Front, the war effort began to crumble. In 1916, the Austrian prime minister was assassinated, and the people became ever more weary of food shortages and slaughter. In 1917,

Austria's new emperor, Karl I, failed in a bid to make a separate peace with the Allies.

In Russia, the so-called February Revolution (according to the Russian calendar; it was actually in March 1917 according to the Western calendar) overthrew the ruling Tsar Nicholas II. The new government attempted to continue fighting, but soon Russian troops began to desert and go home. Germany allowed communist exiles, including the leading revolutionary, V. I. Lenin, to cross their territory and return to Russia. Radical communists known as Bolsheviks seized power in a further revolution in October 1917 (November by the Western calendar). Russia pulled out of the war and was torn apart by civil war, to be reborn in 1922 as the communist Soviet Union.

An Australian soldier carries his wounded comrade to a beach in Gallipoli.

SOURCE

REVOLUTIONARY DECREE

"The Workers' and Peasants' Government ... proposes to all warring peoples and their governments to begin at once negotiations leading to a just democratic peace. ... A peace for which the great majority of wearied, tormented, and war-exhausted toilers and laboring classes of all belligerent countries are thirsting, a peace which the Russian workers and peasants have so loudly and insistently demanded since the overthrow of the Tsar's monarchy, such a peace the government considers to be an immediate peace without annexations (i.e., without the seizure of foreign territory and the forcible annexation of foreign nationalities) and without indemnities [compensations] ... .

We have to fight against the hypocrisy of the governments, which, while talking about peace and justice, actually carry on wars of conquest and plunder."

This decree was published in the Bolshevik paper *Izvestia* the following day. It calls for a ceasefire, leading to an end to the war.

Decree on peace delivered to the Second All-Russia Congress of Soviets of Workers' and Soldiers' Deputies, V. I. Lenin, October 26, 1917 (Russian calendar).

25

The home front

In the cities and countryside of Europe, away from the fighting, life was utterly changed by the war. The struggle of civilians in the war effort became known as the "home front," as if this were a line of battle. In a way it was, for dockers, shipbuilders, nurses, miners, railroad workers, munitions workers, police, and journalists all played an important part in the war.

With so many young men away at the front, women began to take on jobs traditionally done by males. They became bus conductors, factory workers, teachers, bank clerks, secretaries, and administrators. In many countries, female units were recruited to support the armed forces in noncombat roles. Between the February and October Revolutions in 1917, Russia raised women's fighting batallions. The change in women's roles in these years affected public attitudes, and in many countries, helped women in the struggle to win the vote after the war.

A woman operates machinery during her shift at a British munitions factory in about 1915. Factories turned out shells for the front 24 hours a day.

There were food shortages across Europe. Britain encouraged people to grow more themselves. In 1917, a Women's Land Army was founded to help with work on farms. About 23,000 women had enrolled by the end of the war. Food rationing was introduced in the United Kingdom in January 1918. In blockaded Germany, food shortages were extreme as early as 1915, and by 1917, starvation was common. It had a draining effect on morale and led to desperate political protests in which women played a major part.

There was increasing shock and anxiety as it became clear just how many young men were dying at the front. When British soldiers went home on leave back to Blighty (the nickname for the British homeland), they were delighted to see their families, but were reluctant to talk about the grim reality of life at the front. Special laws were passed to censor news, letters, and publications.

Popular shows and songs played in the British music halls kept up morale. Jolly and sentimental songs helped to recruit new troops, but many lyrics had a darker humor and bite to them. Sarcastic and often rude versions were sung by troops at the front. The movie theater was a hugely popular new form of entertainment around the globe. News movies were mostly full of propaganda. Silent comedies helped people forget their troubles as they laughed at stars such as Charlie Chaplin.

A British cartoon attempts to boost morale by suggesting that although newspapers at home are full of doom and gloom, troops on the front are actually cheerful and optimistic.

SONG

"Keep the home fires burning,
While your hearts are yearning,
Though your lads are far away
They dream of home.
There's a silver lining
Through the dark clouds shining,
Turn the dark cloud inside out
'Til the boys come home."

This sentimental song from 1914 kept up spirits on the home front.

Keep the Home Fires Burning music by Ivor Novello, words by Lena Ford.

War and the arts

Some of the most powerful images of the war came from the imagination of artists, writers, and musicians. Some of these were serving soldiers. Others were official war artists, sent to provide a historical record of what they saw. Many painters were not concerned with photographic realism, but with underlying impressions and emotions such as grief and anger.

Dead Sentry in a Trench *was the work of the German artist, Otto Dix (1891–1961), who fought on both the Western and Eastern Fronts.*

German painters included Max Beckmann, who served as a medical orderly. His wartime experiences changed his classical style to distorted, fragmented visions, as in *Die Granate* (*The Shell*, 1915). Alfred Kubin's *Die Kriegsfackel* (*The Torch of War*, 1914) shows the figure of Death burning down houses. A painting by the French

SOURCE

POEM

"What passing-bells for these who
 die as cattle?
Only the monstrous anger of the guns.
Only the stuttering rifles' rapid rattle
Can patter out their hasty orisons.

No mockeries for them; no prayer
 nor bells,
Nor any voice of morning save
 the choirs—
The shrill, demented choirs—of
 wailing shells;
And bugles calling for them from
 sad shires ..."

Siegfried Sassoon's friend, Wilfred Owen, produced some of the most moving poetry of all. He was killed one week before the end of the war. This poem by Owen was one of nine set to music by the composer Benjamin Britten in his *War Requiem*, 1962.

Wilfred Owen, *Anthem for Doomed Youth*, 1917.

artist, Pierre Bonnard, *Un village en ruines près de Ham (A Village in Ruins near Ham,* 1917) shows soldiers near the front line.

Paintings by the English artist, Paul Nash, such as *The Ypres Salient by Night* (1917–18) and the ironically titled *We Are Making a New World* (1918), show landscapes after battle, in complete desolation. In a letter from the Western Front to his wife before the end of the war, Nash wrote *"I am no longer an artist. I am a messenger who will bring back word from the men who are fighting to those who want the war to go on forever. Feeble, inarticulate will be my message, but it will have a bitter truth and may it burn their lousy souls."*

Poets at first praised heroism, but this war held little romance. The Austrian poet, Georg Trakl, commited suicide in 1914. The German poet and dramatist, Ernst Toller, had a breakdown in 1916. The romantic poetry of the English officer and war hero, Siegfried Sassoon, changed to describe the grim reality of the trenches.

Many accounts of the war appeared after 1918. Robert Graves's autobiography *Goodbye to All That* and Ernest Hemingway's novel *A Farewell to Arms,* set on the Italian front, were both published in 1929.

Even after World War II, World War I was still inspiring artists. In 1962, Joseph Losey's movie, *King and Country,* told the harrowing story of a wartime court-martial. The antiwar

FILM POSTER

The year 1929 saw Erich Maria Remarque's internationally popular novel *Im Westen Nichts Neues (All Quiet on the Western Front),* which sold 2.5 million copies in the first 18 months. It was made into a movie in 1930.

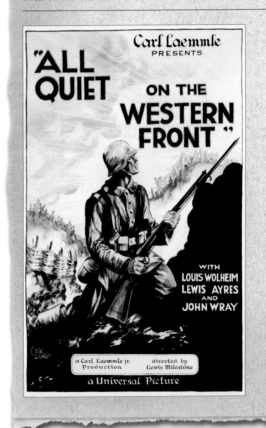

stage musical *Oh What a Lovely War!* (1963, filmed in 1969) was based on popular songs of 1914–18.

Camels and sand

Beyond the shores of Europe, British empire troops were gathering in Cairo and in the heat and dust of the Egyptian desert. Their enemy was the Ottoman empire of the Turks, which controlled much of the Middle East, a region in which Germany was trying to check British power. The Turks had lost territory in Europe and North Africa, and hoped that an alliance with the Central Powers would help to

Troops from the Indian Army guard the Suez Canal, in Egypt, against the Turkish army. India was part of the British empire.

restore their fortunes. The Allied aim was to conquer and share most of the Turkish-ruled lands among themselves.

Middle Eastern oil had become a precious resource. The British fleet had been powered by oil instead of coal since 1911. Britain's first instinct in 1914 was to protect the pipeline of its Anglo-Persian Oil Company. APOC (the forerunner of British Petroleum) also had a 50 percent share in the Turkish Petroleum Company. This led to British and Indian troops attacking

SOURCE

BOOK

"We reached Hesa to find Nasir, with six hundred men, concealed under the cliffs and bushes, afraid of enemy aircraft, which had killed many. One bomb had fallen into a pool while eleven camels had been drinking, and had thrown them all, dead, in a ring about the waterside among torn flowers of oleander … The railroad was still in Nasir's hands … The day of our arrival the Turks sent a force of camel corps, cavalry, and infantry, down to reoccupy Faraifra as a first counterstroke. Nasir at once was up and at them …"

The Hejaz railroad ran from Damascus in Syria, through Transjordan (Jordan) to Medina in Arabia. It had been built by Turkey between 1900 and 1908, with German assistance. In WWI, it came under constant attack from Arab guerrillas.

T. E. Lawrence "of Arabia" in *Seven Pillars of Wisdom* (1922).

and capturing the port of Basra, in Turkish-ruled Mesopotamia (modern Iraq). Turkey responded with a westward offensive, crossing the Sinai desert and launching an attack on the vital shipping route of the Suez Canal, in British-ruled Egypt. The Turks were held back by Indian troops.

British empire troops advanced into Mesopotamia, with heavy loss of life. In 1916, they were defeated by Turkey at the siege of Kut-al-Amara. However, in 1917, the British did take the regional capital, Baghdad. Farther west, British empire troops were struggling through Gaza to capture Palestine and later Syria. British policy was to

support an Arab revolt against Turkish rule across the region. Their agent was a maverick British soldier and scholar named T. E. Lawrence (later known as Lawrence of Arabia). He fought a guerrilla war alongside the Arabs, blowing up train lines, riding camels, and wearing Arab dress.

In return for their support, Britain promised the Arabs future independence. In fact, the French and British partitioned the Middle East for

SOURCE

FILM POSTER

Lawrence of Arabia is an epic movie based on the life of T. E. Lawrence. It was made in 1962 and is about Lawrence's experiences in Arabia in WWI, in particular his attacks on Aqaba and Damascus.

themselves, with the Sykes-Picot agreement of 1916. Britain also made it clear (in the Balfour Declaration, 1917) that it sympathized with Zionists who wanted Jews from other parts of the world to settle in Palestine. These contrary policies were at the root of the conflict dividing the Middle East today.

Around the world

In 1914, the parts of the British empire that had been colonized and settled by the British and Europeans were mostly self-governing "dominions." They included Canada, New Zealand, Newfoundland, the Commonwealth of Australia, and the Union of South Africa. These lands were still bound by British foreign policy and so joined the war at its start. Their troops undertook heavy fighting in Europe and the Middle East, and their sacrifice added to their feelings of independence from the "mother country." Australia and Canada each sent over 450,000 troops overseas, and New Zealand, over 112,000. The dominions also supplied additional helpers, such as engineers, nurses, and timber workers.

Observers often ignored the important role played by Caribbeans, Africans, and Asians in the conflict. Racism was widespread at this time, and many imperial rulers believed that the people they ruled and who fought for them were inferior. In fact, these men fought bravely in some of the most difficult situations. The British West Indies Regiment was 15,600 strong, fighting in Palestine and providing support on the Eastern and Italian Fronts.

In many European colonies, nationalists hoped that war service would later be rewarded with civil rights or independence. This did not begin to happen until after WWII ended. Many Algerians fought for France on the Western Front. In Britain's Kenya colony, in East Africa, indigenous or native peoples were among the troops fighting the Germans across the dusty savanna of Tanganyika. The German colonies of Kamerun and Togoland were occupied by Britain and France with Nigerian and Senegalese troops. The Dominion of South Africa, part of the British empire, invaded German southwest Africa (now Namibia). Some Afrikaners (white South Africans of Dutch descent) did not support Britain, but it was an Afrikaner, General Jan Smuts, who led the British empire's African campaigns.

Cavalry of the Indian Army exercises at Querrieu in Picardy, northern France.

Japanese troops occupy the German-controlled territory of Qingdao in China.

Asia played a major part in the war. About 1.3 million troops and laborers from British-ruled India (which included what are now Pakistan and Bangladesh) served in Europe and Asia. Other fighters included Gurkha troops from Nepal and Thais from Siam (Thailand). Men from French Indo-China (Vietnam, Laos, and Cambodia) supported the war effort by working in French factories. Japanese naval vessels protected Allied convoys as far away as the Mediterranean Sea, and Japanese troops took control of many Pacific islands formerly ruled by Germany.

ULTIMATUM

"In order to secure firm and enduring peace in Eastern Asia … the Imperial Japanese Government sincerely believes it to be its duty to give advice to the Imperial German Government to carry out the following two propositions:

(1) Withdraw immediately from Japanese and Chinese waters the German men-o'-war and armed vessels of all kinds, and to disarm at once those which cannot be withdrawn.

(2) To deliver on a date not later than September 15th, to the Imperial Japanese authorities, without condition or compensation, the entire leased territory of Kiao-chau, with a view to the eventual restoration of the same to China."

From the start, WWI was being played out in the Far East as well as Europe. When Germany rejected this Japanese ultimatum or warning, the German-ruled port of Qingdao (Tsingtao) in Kiao-chau in China was attacked by Japanese troops. Chinese soldiers fought alongside the Germans. *Men-o'-war* is an old-fashioned term for warships. After the war, Qingdao was not returned to China as originally promised.

Ultimatum given by Count Okuma, Japanese Prime Minister, August 15, 1914.

"Over there!"

Over There! was a popular American song of 1917, with the line "The Yanks are coming." And so they were. The United States of America entered the war on April 6, 1917, not as a member of the Allied forces, but as an independent Associated Power.

The original U.S. policy had been isolationist, staying out of the war, but trying to mediate between the two sides. Most Americans had seen the war as a struggle between the imperial powers, and did not realize that the U.S.A. itself had become such a power. Some powerful Americans had always been prowar and their voices became louder after the sinking of the *Lusitania* in 1915 (see page 19). German submarine attacks became a major reason for the U.S.A. joining the war. Another was a German statement (the Zimmermann telegram) that if the U.S.A. did enter the war, Germany would seek an alliance with Mexico to help that country regain lost territory such as Texas, New Mexico, and Arizona. Mexico refused the offer, but the U.S.A. naturally regarded the proposal as a hostile act by Germany.

President Woodrow Wilson saw the war as a chance to secure a peaceful future for liberal democracy, by opposing the militaristic and conservative forces of the Central Powers. However, Wilson did bring in far from liberal laws to gag the U.S. antiwar movement. Jingoism soon ran riot, as it had in Europe in 1914. As in Britain, citizens of German descent were harassed and abused.

U.S. entry had always been feared by the Central Powers. Germany made a desperate bid to break through on the

SOURCE

POSTER

This was a U.S. recruitment poster created in 1917 by James Montgomery Flagg.

U.S. troops on the March. Americans would make up about 2 percent of those killed fighting the Central Powers in the war.

Western Front before U.S. troops could be shipped to Europe. Yet it was clear that the U.S. arrival marked the beginning of the end for Germany. The U.S.A. had vast wealth and manpower. Its troops were not yet exhausted and disillusioned.

American soldiers were nicknamed "doughboys," although no one is quite sure why. African-American troops were subjected to racism, being segregated from whites. Troops dressed in khaki and wore broad-brimmed felt hats, replaced by steel helmets in battle. Infantry carried Springfield rifles.

The first troops of the American Expeditionary Force reached France in June 1917. By the end of the war, they would number two million. Major U.S. campaigns included St. Mihiel in September 1917, and the Meuse-Argonne offensive from September 1918 until the end of the war.

SOURCE

POLITICAL JUDGEMENTS

"The Allies must not be beaten. It would mean the triumph of Autocracy over Democracy; the shattering of all our moral standards; and a real, though it may seem remote, peril to our independence and institutions."

Robert Lansing sums up the case for the war. *Autocracy* means rule by a single person, generally a repressive monarch or dictator. This argument is still used by historians who believe that WWI was justified.

U.S. Secretary of State Robert Lansing, January 28, 1917.

"And all this madness, all this rage, all this flaming death of our civilization and our hopes, has been brought about because a set of official gentlemen, living luxurious lives, mostly stupid, and all without imagination or heart, have chosen that it should occur rather than that any one of them should suffer some infinitesimal [immeasurably small] rebuff to his country's pride."

This argument by Bertrand Russell sums up the argument against the war. It is still the opinion of many historians who see the war as a futile clash between rival empires.

Bertrand Russell, 1914.

The guns fall silent

By 1918, the war was eating up money and lives. Public opinion in Europe varied from weariness to anger or fear. An epidemic of influenza (flu) began to rage through Europe in 1918, eventually killing even more people than the war itself.

In August 1918, the Allies began a final push, the Hundred Days offensive. The Germans began to retreat, and 100,000 prisoners were taken. On September 29, 1918, Bulgaria signed an armistice, or ceasefire. Austria-Hungary was defeated by Italy at the battle of Vittorio Veneto at the end of October, bringing an end to the southern war and the rule of the ancient Habsburg dynasty. On October 30, the Turkish government signed an armistice agreement on board a British warship in Greece.

Germany was isolated. Its High Seas Fleet was ordered to do battle with the British, but refused to sail. The naval mutiny at Kiel in November triggered communist uprisings in Munich and Berlin. The German

emperor, Kaiser Wilhelm II, was forced to abdicate and went into exile in the Netherlands. A republic was declared.

An armistice between the Germans and the Allies was signed in a railroad car in the Compiègne Forest in Picardy, France, at 5 a.m. on November 11, 1918. After a massive exchange of fire, the guns fell silent on the Western Front—around the eleventh hour of the eleventh day of the eleventh month, an event still commemorated at remembrance ceremonies around the world. Troops could not believe the ceasefire would last. Many just fell

The Daily Mirror of London announces the end of war on November 11, 1918.

Jubilant French crowds and troops come onto the streets to celebrate the November 11 Armistice.

asleep, exhausted. On the streets of London, Paris, and U.S. cities, cheering crowds waved Allied flags. The wave of joy and relief was tempered by grief. Many soldiers had died in the last few weeks of the war.

In Germany, which was experiencing defeat and famine, there was relief but little joy. The governing Social Democrats struggled to gain the upper hand over revolutionary councils of workers and soldiers. Radical antiwar socialists called Spartacists came out on the streets of Berlin. Their leaders, Rosa Luxemburg and Karl Liebknecht, were captured and murdered. There were street battles as embittered ex-army officers and monarchists formed right-wing militias, known as the *Freikorps*. They claimed they had been let down by the generals—"stabbed in the back"—and that Germany should have continued fighting.

NEWSPAPER

"WITH THE BRITISH ARMIES IN FRANCE, Nov. 11

Last night, for the first time since August in the first year of the war, there was no light of gunfire in the sky, no sudden stabs of flame through darkness, no spreading glow above black trees, where for four years of nights human beings were smashed to death. The Fires of Hell had been put out."

The New York Times, exclusive by Philip Gibbs, 1918.

Counting the cost

The last fatalities of the war occurred in June 1919, during the peace negotiations. The German fleet had been impounded in Scapa Flow, Scotland. The fleet was scuttled (intentionally sunk) by defiant German crews. Nine were killed when the British realized what was happening.

World War I had been the deadliest conflict the world had ever known. Even more people would die in World War II, just 21 years later. However, the carnage of the 1914–18 conflict is still shocking to us today, especially when so many lives were lost in useless battles over just a few acres of mud. Farmers' plows in France and Belgium still turn up the remains of the fighting—bones and brass buttons and shell cases.

The neatly tended graveyards of the old Western Front present a seemingly endless panorama of white crosses.

SOURCE

MEMOIR

"Yesterday I visited the battlefield of last year. The place was scarcely recognizable. Instead of a wilderness of ground torn up by shell, the ground was a garden of wild flowers and tall grasses. Most remarkable of all was the appearance of many thousands of white butterflies which fluttered around. It was as if the souls of the dead soldiers had come to haunt the spot where so many fell. It was eerie to see them. And the silence! It was so still that I could almost hear the beat of the butterflies' wings."

A British officer, 1919.

War graves in France: every cross represents a lost son, brother, or father.

In almost every village and market town across Europe, there are memorials to the dead of this war. Australian and New Zealand families still travel across the world to pay their respects at Gallipoli, as do Americans to visit the war graves of their dead in Europe. In 1920, a tomb to "the Unknown Soldier," representing all the undiscovered and unidentified dead of the British empire, was placed in London's Westminster Abbey. France placed a similar tomb under the Arc de Triomphe in Paris in 1921.

The effects of the casualties on postwar society were devastating. A whole generation of young men did not come home to marry and raise families. They were not there to work, to create, to take part in society. Those who returned home wounded were often confined to wheelchairs, blind, suffering from shellshock, or haunted by memories of the trenches. Often forgotten are the millions of civilians who also died during the war, whether in the shelled villages of the Eastern Front or in the massacres of Armenians in Turkey.

The nature of war had changed during the course of these years. In the period between the wars, there was a rise in pacifism and internationalism. This lessened with the onset of WWII, but rose again in the 1950s with concern over the development of nuclear weapons.

CASUALTY FIGURES OF WORLD WAR I

ALLIED AND ASSOCIATED POWERS:

- Total population: 789.9 million
- Total military deaths: 5,696,056
- Total military wounded: 12,809,280
- Total civilian deaths: 3,674,757

Nations that suffered the worst death toll:
1 Russia, 2 France, 3 Italy, 4 United Kingdom, 5 Romania

CENTRAL POWERS:

- Total population: 143.1 million
- Total military deaths: 4,024,397
- Total military wounded: 8,419,533
- Total civilian deaths: 5,193,000

Nations that suffered the worst death toll:
1 Ottoman Empire, 2 Germany, 3 Austria-Hungary, 4 Bulgaria

TOTALS (including neutral nations):

- Total population of areas affected: 941 million
- Total military deaths: 9,720,453
- Total civilian deaths: 8,867,757
- Total all deaths: 18,588,210

* Figures do not include overseas empire casualties.

The terms of peace

The Armistice of 1918 was just a ceasefire agreement. The full terms of the settlement were not decided until the Paris Peace Conference of 1919. These discussions resulted in five separate treaties, dealing with Germany, Austria, Hungary, Bulgaria, and Turkey. The German peace agreement was known as the Treaty of Versailles.

The defeated nations were not represented in Paris. They were simply presented with the decisions of the victors. The most powerful negotiators were President Woodrow Wilson of the U.S.A., French Prime Minister Georges Clemenceau, British Prime Minister David Lloyd George, and Italian Prime Minister Vittorio Orlando. Wilson's most important proposal was the creation of a League of Nations, an international treaty organization designed to prevent further conflict.

Germany was to disarm and become a democratic republic. Its overseas empire was dismantled, as were the territories of the Ottoman Empire. Rule of these various colonies was to be mandated (licensed for a given term) by the League of Nations. Mandates were issued to Britain, France, Belgium, South Africa, Japan, Australia, and New Zealand. Under this system, Britain was now to govern Palestine and Iraq, and France was to govern Lebanon and Syria.

Clemenceau, Wilson, and Lloyd George (left to right) after signing the Treaty of Versailles on June 28, 1919. The state of war with Germany was at last ended.

Borders were redrawn on the map of Europe. New nations included Czechoslovakia and a re-formed Polish republic. Italy gained territory from Austria. France was determined that it would never again be invaded by Germany. It took over the border region of Alsace, where it expelled many Germans and banned the use of the German language. French troops occupied the Rhineland, in western Germany. Germany was ordered to pay heavy financial penalties as compensation, called reparations.

The Peace Conference Committee meets to draw up the covenant of the League of Nations.

The other Allies were concerned that the French penalties were too harsh and would have the opposite effect to those intended and cause a rise in nationalism and resentment. Germany was presented with the treaty and given no choice but to sign. It did so, under protest, on June 28, 1919.

The Germans were not the only ones unhappy with the terms of the Peace of Paris. Japan was not treated equally with the other victors, and felt that it had been snubbed for racist reasons.

COVENANT

"Any war or threat of war, whether immediately affecting any of the Members of the League or not, is hereby declared a matter of concern to the whole League, and the League shall take any action that may be deemed wise and effectual to safeguard the peace of nations. In case any such emergency should arise, the Secretary General shall, on the request of any Member of the League, forthwith summon a meeting of the Council."

The League of Nations was intended as a mechanism to enforce international law in the interests of peace. It was established in 1919 and was based in Geneva, in neutral Switzerland. It was given little real power and failed to prevent WWII. At its height, it had 58 member nations.

Article 11, Covenant of the League of Nations.

British delegates argued against a proposed amendment to the League of Nations charter that called for equality between the races. They feared that it would undermine the operation of the British empire. Nationalists from Allied colonies lobbied the Peace Conference demanding self-rule, with no success.

The aftermath

Society after the war was greatly changed. There was a decline in social stuffiness and tradition. This was an exciting new age of jazz, sports, radio, movies, and motor cars. Many women had greater freedom and power than before the war. However, the new world order was built on shaky political and economic foundations. In the 1920s, there was economic depression in Britain and in Germany. The U.S.A.'s financial institutions collapsed in the Wall Street Crash of 1929, and few parts of the world escaped the economic hardship that followed. However, the children and grandchildren of those who fought in WWI did live to see better times.

The war did not succeed in Woodrow Wilson's aim of making the world "safe for democracy." Nor was it

Hungry men line up for food in New York City during the economic depression that followed the Wall Street Crash of 1919.

"a war to end all wars," for the Peace of Paris contained the seeds of future conflict. In Germany, the harsh terms of the treaty played into the hands of the small Nazi Party, a racist organization that aimed to rearm, seize power, and reverse the humiliation of WWI. Japan was left with ambitions to create its own empire in the Pacific. These factors contributed to WWII.

Woodrow Wilson was awarded a Nobel Peace Prize in 1919. Sadly, he suffered a stroke and died in 1921. With Congress controlled by Wilson's opponents in the Republican Party, the U.S. government failed to ratify the Treaty of Versailles. The U.S.A. never joined the League of Nations. This greatly reduced the organization's ability to prevent conflict in the coming years. In 1945, the League of Nations was replaced by a new organization, the United Nations.

The peacemakers of 1919 rearranged the old empires, but did not address the basic injustices of the imperial system. The right to self-rule by colonial peoples would be a major cause of conflict in the twentieth century. Vietnamese lobbyists were cold-shouldered at Versailles, yet the long colonial war in French Indo-China led directly to the Vietnam War, fought by the U.S.A. in the 1960s. The Russian revolutions of 1917 and communism in Russia were remarkable events in history and eventually led to a period of international conflict and tension called the Cold War (1940s–90).

After the war, what next? David Lloyd George, the British Prime Minister, addresses a crowd at the train station in Lampeter, Wales.

SPEECH

"What is our task? To make Britain a fit country for heroes to live in."

David Lloyd George made this political speech at Wolverhampton on November 23, 1918, just after the Armistice. In reality, many soldiers who came home soon found themselves unemployed and hungry. Out of uniform, they were rarely treated as heroes.

David Lloyd George, the U.K. Prime Minister, 1918. Speech from *The Times*, November 25, 1918.

Lessons of history

Is it worthwhile looking back at this war from the twenty-first century and asking ourselves some questions? Is war ever morally justifiable, and if so, does it matter how destructive it is? Can it ever be acceptable to refuse to serve your country as a soldier, or to disobey orders? Is it ever justified for a nation to bomb civilians? Is it different from an individual bombing civilians?

Did the arms race before WWI provide countries with security, or make matters more dangerous? Could the rush to war have been avoided by diplomacy? Could international law have been used to change the way in which this war was conducted, and how could it be used to prevent conflict today? Was WWI unique, or does it have similarities with WWII? Can we draw any general conclusions from studying it? Could Europe again break apart in such a war, or is it impossible given modern economic and political ties?

The debates about WWI war go on, as does the remembrance of those who died. Perhaps the best way to honor the young people who were killed at the start of the last century is to prevent a world war from occurring again.

Poppies flower in a French field. Poppies grew all over the old trenches at the end of the war and became a symbol of remembrance.

1914

June 28	Assassination of Austrian Archduke at Sarajevo.
August 1–4	Outbreak of World War I: Germany invades Belgium.
September 5–10	French victory at First Battle of the Marne.
September 14 –November 2	First Battle of Ypres.
October 29	Ottoman empire joins the Central Powers.
October 31 –November 7	Japanese attack Germans in Qingdao (Tsingtao), China.
December 25	Unofficial Christmas truce on parts of the Western Front.

1915

March 11	Britain blockades German fleet.
April 22 –May 25	Second Battle of Ypres.
April 25	Gallipoli landings, Turkey.
May 7	Sinking of the *Lusitania* by a German U-boat.
May 23	Italy joins Allies in breach of treaty commitments.
June 23	Start of Italian battles along the Isonzo River.
December 28	Allied evacuation of Gallipoli.
February 10	Conscription begins in the United Kingdom.

1916

April 29	Turks defeat British at Kut-al-Amara (in present-day Iraq).
May 31 –June 1	Naval battle of Jutland between Germany and Britain.
July–November	Somme offensive, Western Front.
August	Romania joins the Allies.
September 15	British use tanks on the Western Front.

1917

January 19	The Zimmermann telegram: Germany proposes Mexican alliance.
March 11	Britain captures Baghdad.
March 15	February Revolution in Russia, Tsar Nicholas II abdicates.
April 6	The United States joins the war on side of the Allies.
June 26	First U.S. troops arrive in France.
June 16 –November 10	Passchendaele offensive, Belgium.
November 7	October Revolution in Russia; Bolsheviks seize power.
November 20	Tank battle of Cambrai won by British.
December 3	Russian–German Armistice.

1918

March 3	Treaty of Brest-Litovsk, peace between Russia and Central Powers.
June 15	Second Battle of the Marne.
June 15–July	Battle of the Piave River, Italy.
August 8	The Hundred Days offensive.
September 29	Bulgarian Armistice.
October 30	Turkish Armistice.
November 3	German fleet mutinies at Kiel.
November 9	German Kaiser Wilhelm II abdicates.
November 11	Armistice signed between the Germans and the Allies.

1919

January 18	Peace Conference opens in Paris.
June 28	Signing of the Treaty of Versailles.

GLOSSARY

Abdicate
To resign from being king, queen, or emperor.

Anglicize
To alter a name or a custom to an English form.

Armistice
An agreed ceasefire or truce in a war.

Arms race
When nations compete to acquire more armaments than their rivals.

Artillery
Guns, mortars, or other machines used to fire shells, rockets, or other missiles.

Cannon fodder
A sarcastic term for soldiers sent into battle by their commanders without due care for their lives.

Censor
To delete passages of a communication or literary text, especially for reasons of politics, security, or morality.

Communist
A radical or revolutionary socialist who supports a state-controlled or -directed economy, belonging to a political party that claims to represent the working class.

Conscientious objector
Someone who refuses to fight as a matter of conscience or principle.

Conscript
To order people to join the armed forces.

Conservative
Opposed to political reform or radical change.

Constitution
The set of laws that determine how a country is organized and governed.

Court-martialed
To be tried in front of a military court.

Empire
Many different countries or territories ruled by a single government.

Ethical
Concerning what is right as opposed to what is wrong.

Grenade
A small bomb thrown by hand or fired from a gun or hand-held launcher.

Guerrilla
An irregular fighter who avoids pitched battle, using surprise attacks and sabotage to wear down the enemy.

Huns
1) Asiatic warriors who attacked Eastern and Central Europe in the 300s and 400s CE.
2) A term of abuse used to describe Germans before and during WWI.

Imperialism
Policy of the rule and economics of empires.

Isolationist
Following a foreign policy of noninvolvement or nonintervention.

Jingoism
Populist, aggressive, or warlike patriotism.

Liberal
Politically progressive or free-minded.

Lobby
To urge politicians to take a particular course of action, or adopt a certain policy.

Magazine
1) A store for explosives.
2) A metal container from which bullets are loaded into a rifle.

Mine
To bury bombs across an area of land or to float them in the sea, so that they explode on contact with the enemy.

Mortar
A short, broad cannon used for firing shells at a high angle.

Nationalist
1) Someone who campaigns for nationhood, by calling for independence, a union of small territories, or separation from a larger territory.
2) Someone who places great importance on nationality.

Pacifist
Someone who opposes all armed conflict, someone who campaigns for peace.

Parapet
The front edge of a trench. Launching an attack over the parapet was called "going over the top."

Patriotic
Loving one's country, eager to serve one's country.

Periscope
A mirrored tube allowing one to see safely over the edge of a trench, or above the surface of the sea from a submarine.

Ratify
To confirm an agreement formally, or to give it full legal status.

Right-wing
Opposed to liberalism, socialism, or communism.

Shell shock
Any of various disabilities caused by stress and trauma in battle.

Sniper
An expert rifleman trained to pick off individual targets as they present themselves.

Socialist
Someone who supports public ownership and opposes conservatism.

Xenophobia
Fear or hatred of foreigners.

FURTHER INFORMATION AND WEB SITES

FURTHER READING

America in World War I by Richard Worth (World Almanac Library, 2006)

Private Peaceful by Michael Morpurgo (Scholastic Paperbacks, 2006)

World War I by Simon Adams (DK Children, 2007)

WEB SITES

Due to the changing nature of Internet links, Rosen Publishing has developed an online list of Web Sites related to the subject of this book. This site is regularly updated. Please use this link to access this list: http://www.rosenlinks.com/doc/wwar

INDEX

Numbers in **bold** refer to illustrations.